BEEKEEPING ON TWO FRONTS
1914 – 1918

Compiled from the British Bee Journals of the time by Stuart Ching

NORTHERN BEE BOOKS

BEEKEEPING ON TWO FRONTS 1914 – 1918
© Stuart Ching

All rights reserved. No part of this publication may be reproduced, stored in a retrieval system, transmitted in any form or by any means electronic, mechanical, including photocopying, recording or otherwise without prior consent of the copyright holders.

ISBN 978-1-908904-56-0

Published by Northern Bee Books, 2014
Scout Bottom Farm
Mytholmroyd
Hebden Bridge
HX7 5JS (UK)

Design and Artwork, D&P Design and Print

Printed by Lightning Source UK

BEEKEEPING ON TWO FRONTS
1914 – 1918

Compiled from the British Bee Journals of the time by Stuart Ching

NORTHERN BEE BOOKS

BEEKEEPING ON TWO FRONTS
1914 – 1918

Compiled from the British Bee Journals of the time by Stuart Ching

When one thinks of this period one is naturally drawn to the armed conflict raging on the continent and elsewhere which came to be known as the Great War or ironically "the war to end all wars." Records show that bee-keepers were not isolated from this and, indeed, they show that not only did they serve but some became casualties.

However, many beekeepers were involved in another war on what was called the "Home Front" and were involved in fighting the dreaded "Isle of Wight" disease. This disease wiped out thousands of honeybee colonies during this period.

This work relies on the narratives of three people.

Part One is reported by Sgt Atwell who fought in France throughout the War. He wrote to the Journal despite being heavily involved in the major battles of the conflict. He also survived the War and continued to write articles for the Journal but these articles were now restricted to beekeeping. There is no indication in the Journal where Sgt Atwell lived.

Part Two deals with the problems of beekeeping in the UK. Don Wilson of Belper was a bee "expert" at the outbreak of the War. He wrote a series of articles for the Journal entitled "Notes from Derbyshire" and was well-known as a lecturer on beekeeping subjects. When Don was conscripted into the Royal Engineers towards the end of the War, Tom Sleight of Clay Cross took over his column. Both survived the war and continued to contribute to the journal.

(Stuart Ching has been the Editor of the Nottinghamshire Beekeepers' Association newsletter since 1994. Though not now an active beekeeper he takes a great interest in the history of beekeeping particularly of his native county. He furthers his interests in local history by being a volunteer with the Community Archaeologists of Nottinghamshire carrying out 'digs' in many parts of the county.)

BEEKEEPING ON TWO FRONTS

PART ONE

BEES AT THE FRONT
AG Atwell, Lance Corporal later promoted to Sergeant

December 10th 1914

The following letter, which we have received from "the Front," will, we are sure be read with interest, and our readers will join with us in wishing the writer a safe and speedy return to his home and the bees. His action in fixing up the hives is another instance of the freemasonry existing among bee-keepers, not only in our own country, but the world over. Reading between the lines we have no doubt Mr Atwell ran considerable personal risk while performing his kindly action. As the letter is stamped " Passed by the Censor, we print it in full.

With the British Expeditionary Force

December 1st 1914.

Dear Sirs—I thought I should like to write you a few lines to let you know how much I have appreciated the articles in your little Journal, which I have had sent me regularly from home ever since I have been on active service. I left England in August and have been through all the big engagements with my regiment. I have often read the Journal under a perfect hell of heavy German artillery fire, often not knowing if the next second would be the last one.

However, I have been one of the lucky ones and have steered clear so far, and if I am spared to see England again I hope to give the readers of the Journal some very interesting stories of how their fellow bee-keepers (who are unfortunate enough to have their apiaries within the area of war) have suffered. I have seen apiaries destroyed by shell fire, I have seen them after they have been looted by the Germans, and I have picked up empty skeps on the roadside with a few bees still hovering around their home. Only a few days ago I came across a bee house at a farm which had been evacuated sometime. It was within three-quarters of a mile of the German firing line.

Upon examination I found that two of the skeps had been knocked over on to the ground mouth upwards. They were both crowded with bees and had not been much disturbed. I expect the appearance of so many bees had somewhat frightened the intruder. I managed to get them back on their stand all right with six others which were undisturbed.

The skeps were large, crammed full of comb and honey and heavy in bees. I only hope the owner will find them all right when he returns and will reap a double harvest next year to make up for the one he has left behind this. I may mention that when I found the bees the ground was thick with snow and a cold sleet was falling. German bullets were whistling around and as the apiary was somewhat exposed I had to undergo some risk when getting the skeps in place again. Space and time will not permit me to tell very much now of the sights I have seen here, but I hope with the Editor's permission to write them up at a later date if I am spared to do so.

I should like before I close to give the readers of the Journal a short account of my own bees, as I think I have been extremely lucky with them. I started bee-keeping last year, but of course did not get much surplus, as I did not know anything about them then and really started too late. However, I bought two stocks in a double hive, one swarm in May, which I divided later, and several skeps of driven bees which I had to drive myself without any personal instruction. I made two good stocks of these. I wintered them well, giving them plenty of food during the winter and spring.

Things, however, did not turn out so rosy as I had anticipated, for when I examined them in the spring I found that I had foul brood in four lots (the double hive and two single), only two stocks were apparently healthy. But my troubles were not yet over. Later on bees were dropping around the hives. I sent several packets of dead bees to the "B.B.J." Office.

This was the verdict: Bees are suffering from "Isle of Wight" disease. I was in despair. I thought of making a bonfire of the whole lot and forgetting that there was such a thing on the earth as a bee. I pondered over matters. Every hive in the district had been cleared out with "Isle of Wight" Disease previous to my bringing my six stocks there in the autumn of 1913. I couldn't be a menace to anyone else, and so I decided to give the bees a chance.

One stock, a Carnolian lot, was so bad with foul brood that I thought it best to destroy that one at least, and a second one I shook from the frames, which I burnt, making an artificial swarm of the bees. I transferred the remaining colonies to clean hives well scrubbed with carbolic acid, putting the bees from the double hive into separate hives. I now had five stocks of hybrid bees, one of course being backward owing to my having to re-hive them.

I used 'Apicure' for the foul brood, but nothing beyond the disinfecting for the "Isle of Wight" Disease. This happened about the beginning of April. From this time onwards there was a decided change for the better, and this is the marvelous result: increased from five to fourteen vigorous stocks and took 500lbs. of extracted and 205 sections of surplus honey. This would make a total of over 710lbs. of honey, as most of the sections weighed over a pound.

I have not been at home to winter the bees, so they have been packed down on ten frames, and there must still be a considerable amount of honey left with them. I might say that the increase was made before I left for the war in August, and the purchase of a quantity of drawnout comb added greatly to the harvest. It is also a splendid heather district and most of the hives were well prepared for this when I left, being strong and headed by young queens which I reared myself.

My success is also greatly due to my wife, who, with the assistance of a neighbour, so ably managed the heather flow with practically no previous experience. I am only hoping for one thing now as regards my bees, and that is that I shall be home early enough in the spring to try and go even one better than I have done this season. With fraternal greetings to my fellow bee-keepers at home, I beg to remain, dear Sirs, yours very sincerely,

Lance-Corporal A. G. Atwell.

P.S.—Will you kindly excuse the scribble and composition in this letter? It is difficult writing at the front.

A Queen Bee from "The Front."

March 11th 1915

You will no doubt be rather surprised to receive a queen bee so early in the year as this, and perhaps be more surprised still when you find that she has come from " the Front." As a matter of fact, I've saved her from the Germans. Her eleven other sisters on their big frames, and the hives, have been blown to pieces. The hive I have taken this one from was badly knocked about, all the tops of the frames being exposed to the weather and most of the honey granulated with the cold, yet in such adverse circumstances as these she had a nice patch of brood and eggs, with not a trace of disease so far as I could see. To have left the bees there would mean simply leaving them to die, either by exposure to the weather or the visit of other German shells, which have demolished every house in the village and also the fine old church, which has been a special target for the Huns. I know I am sending you the queen at a rather awkward time, but I thought that (if she arrives alive) you may find some way of preserving her and thus save the last remnant of the fine old French apiary. The strain of bees must be very prolific, as they have such huge brood frames to keep going. I shall have more to tell you of this apiary later.   Lance-Corporal AG Atwell.

[Unfortunately our correspondent placed a small piece of comb containing honey in the box with the bees, and during their journey they became covered with the honey. This, coupled with the cold, was too much for them. The queen was just alive and also five of the workers, but the former was dead ten minutes after the box was opened, although she was promptly warmed near the fire. The five workers became quite lively.   Eds.BBJ]

With the Bees at the Front

August 2nd 1915

AG Atwell with French beekeeper

Where possible I have given the dates and names of places, although I have not always been able to do this, owing, sometimes, to not having made the proper entries in my diary, and at other times because it would be forbidden for military reasons. If I had been in possession of a camera I could have taken some most interesting photographs, but as such a thing is not allowed by the authorities, I have done the next best thing and brought away many souvenirs. Some of these consisted of pieces of heavy shells, etc., and it was with great difficulty that I managed to carry them about with me for several months before I could get them safely home.

I had originally intended to relate my experiences after the war, but as the end seems still a long way off, and as I feel that my story would prove more attractive if written in the trenches, I have decided to do it "right now," as the Americans say, and only trust that my adventures will be as interesting on paper to my readers as they were in reality to myself. It may be as well to say that I am writing these lines within a hundred yards of the German positions, where we are using an old cellar (all that remains of a house) for our first-aid regimental dressing station, of which I am in charge.

The troops in one of our front line trenches are only a few yards from the Germans, and can shout to one another quite easily. Continuous fighting with bombs, hand grenades, and trench mortars is going on there, and I am continually being called away, even while writing these lines, to attend some one who has been hit, often finding them past any aid that can be rendered them in this world. This is a spot which has seen some of the most severe fighting, and was actually in the hands of the Germans a few months ago.

It is just over twelve months ago now that war was declared by England against Germany, and yet the suspense of those few awful days which preceded the declaration hangs in my memory as if it were yesterday and ranks in my mind with some of the worst which I have experienced out here.

Of course, domestic affairs naturally came first, but next to them the bees, and as it is the bees that I intend writing about, I will leave other matters out. When the war came I had sixteen stocks all nicely fixed up and bringing in loads of honey, but being a reservist of the first class I was called up immediately, and had to leave all my bees just as I was beginning to reap the benefit of my work of the previous spring and winter. However, I resolved that when I got to France I would keep my eyes open and see what bee-keeping was like on that side of the Channel. That my observations have not been in vain I think the following story will prove, and although most of my adventures have been attended with some risk, it has really made them more exciting, and has often passed away a few weary hours and turned my mind, for a little while at least, from the horrors of this terrible war.

THE EMBARKATION

It was on August 12th, 1914, that I embarked with my regiment, the 1st South Wales Borderers. We disembarked without mishap, and after a rest of a few hours we marched through the town and arrived at our camp on the top of the cliffs at 5.30 the following morning. Although it was only just breaking day as we came through the town, the windows above the shops and cafes were crowded with people, most of them still clad in their night attire but anxious to catch their first glimpse of the English soldiers and to shout out a welcome, which at that time very few of us could understand. Of the few days that we stayed at the camp I have very little to say, only that the weather was extremely hot and we experienced a most violent thunderstorm one night which threatened to carry our tents away. The people also made a great fuss of us and treated us very well during our few days stay there. We entrained again on Saturday, 15th August, and made a twenty hours' journey IN CATTLE TRUCKS.

This was naturally rather trying, but the novelty of the country which we passed through and the fact that we were going to meet the Germans made us forget, to a certain extent, the rather trying experience of representing a box of sardines. We were not very sorry the following day (Sunday) to arrive at our destination, a little village in northern France called Etreause. Here, after disentangling ourselves, we all indulged in a good stretch, which enabled our bodies to once more assume their natural proportions, and then after a rest of a few hours, during which time many enjoyed a bathe in a swift little trout stream, we marched eight or nine miles in the most drenching rain that I have ever experienced to another little village called Leschelle. It was during our few days' stay at this place that I caught sight of my first French apiary. If it could be called such. It was really a two-storied bee house, such as I afterwards found out to be quite common in this part of the country, and which contained several skeps of bees, which were working well.

October 7th 1915

I also saw a long row of straw-covered skeps in the same village later. But unfortunately I had no time for further investigation, as we were kept rather busy with our preparations to meet the Germans, and could I have met the owners of the bees I am afraid I should have found great difficulty in making myself understood, as my knowledge of the French language was not at its best just then.

I may mention that it was on the night of the 19th August that the first post arrived from home, and there were very

few of us who did not get a letter.

Leaving Leschelle on the morning of the 20th we marched the greater part of the day, reaching a little village called

Malgarni, but our stay here was very short, for we were off again early next morning, and were now well on our way

to meet the Germans, who, of course, as everyone knows, were rapidly invading French and Belgian territory. After

another long march in very hot weather we arrived at the village of St. Aubun another short rest and we were off again early next morning ; we had no time to lose then.

Often as we plodded along the dusty roads we could see the tops of a row of rustic skeps sticking above the hedges, and a village would never be passed without I could see one or more of these old-fashioned little apiaries clustered under the hedge or standing under the shelter of the overhanging thatched roof of one of these quaint old whitewashed cottages.

I must not forget to mention the thousands of refugees we were continually passing on the road. These were of all ages, from babies in arms to old men and women of some 80 or 90 years of age, some plodding along carrying a few of their belongings as best they could, others more fortunate were driving along with all the furniture and accoutrements that it was possible for them to pack on their much overloaded wagons; these vehicles ranged from the little cart drawn by a dog to huge wagons to which were harnessed a team of four or six oxen. Everything that had wheels seemed to be in evidence. On many occasions I have seen these old wagons (many of which had not been used for years) break down with their great loads, and the people have had to leave them where they lay, for there was no time to lose.

The booming of the bursting German shells could be heard in the distance, and the black clouds of smoke which could just be seen rising over the horizon meant that another village was being sacrificed to the flames, striking terror to the hearts of the refugees, and spurring the soldiers on to meet this inhuman foe. I think the sight of these miles of fleeing people was one of the saddest that it has ever been, or ever will be, my lot to witness, and I feel it quite beyond me to adequately describe the scene on paper. One little thing more, however. The people were driving almost every living thing from their farms before them - cows, sheep, and pigs; chickens and ducks packed in baskets and slung under the wagons; all were there.

But the bees? They could not very well bring the bees! And so these little apiaries with their healthy workers and their year's stores still intact were left to the mercy of the invaders. Well I remember about this time passing a house, the owners of which were just preparing to leave. Their bundles were ready on the doorstep, and they were only waiting for the master of the house, who was in the garden having a last look at his bees. He had some six to eight large frame-hives there, which, by the way, were supered and must have contained a considerable amount of honey. This was the biggest apiary of frame hives that I had yet seen, and by their appearance the old man must have given a lot of time to them. I should like to have spoken to him, but as we were only marching by I had not the time, but I often wondered afterwards if he ever left his bees.

October 28th 1915

In the afternoon we reached Mauberge and here we rested at the roadside for about four hours. It was at this village that we received our first pay, although we needed very little money, as the people would give us anything. We moved on again to a somewhat larger village for the night, the name of which I have not entered in my diary. We slept in the village square, most of us. The place was also crowded with refugees, who were sleeping for the night anywhere they could find room to lie down. I remember a few wounded being brought to the village: they were chiefly cavalry scouts, and had been wounded in a skirmish with the German outposts.

We moved a little further on the next day, and got into action for the first time. We held out as long as possible against the advancing hordes of Germans, but on Monday, the 24th of August, we were compelled, in the face of greatly superior numbers, to start our retirement. Of course, this was at about the same time that the retirement from Mons took place and our brigade was on one of the flanks and not actually at Mons itself. We were fighting rearguard actions every step, and had some very heavy marching.

We passed through the town of Soissons on Monday, the 31st. We reached the farthest point of our retirement at about 5 o'clock on September 2nd, having been pressed back to within a few miles of Paris. In fact, rumours were current among the troops that we were actually going there to help hold the forts. However, I am glad to say this was not necessary; for, as everyone knows, we turned about and drove the Germans right back to their positions on the Aisne.

During this advance to the Aisne I made the following notes. Started our advance on Thursday, September 3rd; that evening, while resting, was shaved by a lady barber, a refugee. For several days after this I made no entries, but if I remember rightly it was nothing but continual marching, with scarcely any time for food or sleep. On the 8th we passed a lot of our cavalry, men and horses who had been killed while fighting the German rearguard. This commenced the battle of the Marne. For several days we still continued the advance. All the villages we passed through now had been looted by the Germans; shops broken open, wine cellars looted, cattle and poultry killed and eaten, their entrails being thrown about the ground.

It was on the 12th of September that I came across the first looted apiary. Of course, I expect I had passed several such before, but being hidden behind the hedges, etc., it was not always easy to see them in passing. However, the one I mention was standing right in the open, about six yards from description to shut it off from passing traffic. Of the nine or ten hives (or rather straw-thatched skeps) only about two seemed to be undamaged. Others were burst open, exposing both comb and honey, while others, judging by the empty stands, had been carried completely away.

The troops passed this spot pretty quickly, for, of course, the bees were not in the best of tempers. The following day I found a looted skep by the roadside, with a few bees still hovering round. Honey and comb was all gone, and the skep was most likely one of those taken from the road, with no hedge or fence of any apiary I had seen the day before; it was of wicker work, covered with mud and cow dung, and I made a rough sketch of it at the time, a drawing from which I enclose herewith.

November 25th 1915

Our advance still continued, and many and various were the articles left on the roadside by the retreating Germans. Food tins of all descriptions, old worn out boots and clothing, Helmets and broken equipment. Occasionally a few Prisoners would fall into our hands; These were chiefly stragglers who could not keep up with the main force.

We also passed many large wagons and motors, some which had to be abandoned through slight defects, and others which had overturned in their haste to get away, as the roads in places were none too wide, and the ditches on either side often very deep.

One rather sad sight was the number of horses which we passed, either dead or left in a dying condition, caused by the continual work over heavy roads. It was about this time, while resting in a field, that I saw one of the best hornets' nests that I had ever seen, it was built out from the branch of a tree, and I can assure you that none of us felt inclined to meddle with these huge insects, who seemed to be ready to dart at anyone who should venture too near them.

The weather about this time was rather fine for the time of year, and during the warmest part of the day I noticed numbers of bees swarming round the empty jam tins which were thrown away by the troops. These were evidently bees of looted apiaries anxious to get food of any description to make up for their lost stores. It may be interesting to note that they favoured the orange marmalade, the tins from this conserve being absolutely black with them.

On Sunday night, September 13th, we rested in rather a big village, the name of which I think was Boulne. All along the advance the troops had been anxious to clash with the enemy, but none of us thought that the following morning would see us launched in a most terrible fight, and that many of our comrades who laughed and chatted round the camp fire this Sunday night had but a few hours left to them in this life. However, such was the case, for the following morning, after leaving the village a few miles behind us, we dashed right into the enemy near the tiny rustic village of Chevoy Boulne.

The reader might easily imagine a fine autumn day among a beautiful hilly country, shrouded in its autumn splendour of gold and bronze in all their varying degrees. He might also imagine a little old-world village, with thatched and whitewashed cottages and farms and quaint old folk, many of whom had never been more than a dozen miles from their native village. But try as he might, unless he has actually experienced it, he will never be able to imagine the awful experience of going through such a fight. The roar of the guns, the continual whizz of the bullets, the shrapnel bursting all around; that peaceful country of yesterday was today a veritable hell. It seems marvellous that any living thing could exist at all.

Of the horrible sights of the battlefield I will say but little, it could do the reader no good to hear of them, and although they can never be forgotten, they will best be left untold. How the writer ever came through such an ordeal the One above only knows, but on this and four other occasions (of which I shall write later) I have had some of the nearest shaves that it is possible for anyone to undergo. Of course at this time there were no trenches, and dugouts as there are to-day, only such as could be hastily scratched out during the night.

December 9th 1915

Hurricane of shell fire both day and night, and I was kept so busy attending to the continual stream of wounded (I was employed in the first-aid dressing station at that time) that I had no time while in this place to go exploring for beehives, although I have not the slightest doubt that there were plenty about.

I do not know what happened when the Germans came. Vendresse, a little larger and more modern than the last place, gave me many interesting experiences connected with bees. We had been here no longer than a day before one of the stretcher bearers (who had been exploring some of the vacated houses and gardens) came rushing up to me, and vigorously rubbing his nose, which was already showing signs of an unseen aerial attack, shouted out in great excitement: "Bees! Bees!"

Two or three minutes' walk brought us to the garden, which contained a little apiary of some half-dozen skeps, of the same size and shape as the one I illustrated a few weeks ago. One skep was lying on the ground with a cloud of angry bees flying around. This one, my friend told me, he was carrying away when the bees gently reminded him that it wasn't quite such an easy task as he expected, and forced him to drop them, and beat as hasty a retreat as any he had yet experienced during the war.

WITH THE BEES AT THE FRONT. BBJ November 18th 1915

I notice in Sgt. Atwell's Diary he refers to Maubeuge as a village. I remember this place quite well, especially the forts, as a number of fine houses were blown up, possibly due to the fact that they were in the line of fire. Maubeuge, according to the official map of 1909, had a population of 21,520, Louvroil 4,750, and Hautmont 13,125. Both of these places are within three miles of Maubeuge, and on the Maubeuge - Landrecies road. Sgt. Atwell's article is very interesting to me, having been through these places myself. I hope you will excuse writing as I have to lie on my side.

L. Kettle.

Mr. Kettle's correction referring to Maubeuge is certainly quite right, and I was in error in referring to that place as a callage. But not having at all times made full entries and descriptions of places in my diary, and it being over twelve months ago that these events happened, it is often difficult, after the many and varied experiences which I have been through, to give a correct description of all of them, although I must certainly be more careful in the future. However, my readers may rest assured that should I make any error in the description of places, I shall make none with my experiences with the bees, as these stand out as vividly as though they happened yesterday, and, of course, form the most important part of the story. However, I thank our friend for his correction, and shall always be pleased to hear of any more mistakes I may be liable to make under the many difficulties in which I write.

Continuing my story, we found ourselves, after a day of continuous fighting, in the little village of Chivvy Boulne, Here we stayed for a week, my regiment helping to hold a ridge of hills just outside the village. The place was under aat the war, her married daughter lived miles away, and so this old lady - too old to leave her native village was left to her fate. Often when I had a minute to spare during the day I would cross over, and she was always delighted to see me; she would open her little Bible, which she always carried with her, then amidst the thunder of the guns and bursting shells (any one of which might demolish the house at any moment), the old lady would turn to a picture of the Virgin Mary, and pointing above would exclaim, "La Saint Monsieur, La Saint." We had to evacuate the place after a week there, and withdraw to another village called Vendresse. But the old lady, together with a few other old people, stayed behind. I do not know what happened when the Germans came. Vendresse, a little larger and more modern than the last place, gave me many interesting experiences connected with bees.

We had been here no longer than a day before one of the stretcher bearers (who had been exploring some of the vacated houses and gardens) came rushing up to me, and vigorously rubbing his nose, which was already showing signs of an unseen aerial attack, shouted out in great excitement: "Bees! Bees!" Two or three minutes walk brought us to the garden, which contained a little apiary of some half-dozen skeps, of the same size and shape as the one I illustrated a few weeks ago. One skep was lying on the ground with a cloud of angry bees flying around. This one, my friend told me, he was carrying away when the bees gently reminded him that it wasn't quite such an easy task as he expected, and forced him to drop them, and beat as hasty a retreat as any he had yet experienced during the war.

February 17th 1916

We stayed at the Convent of St. Barbara for about eight days, during which time the beautiful village church and most of the houses were destroyed by shellfire. Although the convent was very much exposed, the Germans, for some reason, did not shell it until the night we left.

That awful night I shall never forget. The regiment were being relieved by the French, and by seven o'clock were well on their way back, together with the majority of our stretcher-bearers. The doctor, myself, and two or three men remained behind to look after some wounded for whom we were expecting an ambulance.

However, this never reached us, for about nine o'clock the Germans started an attack on the positions taken over by the French. During this attack they seemed to remember the convent, for they rained shell after shell upon us. These were shells of the heavy type, and any direct hit would have blown up the convent and set it on fire. We simply sat there with the wounded, expecting every moment to be the last.

It was an awful experience; these huge shells, which were being rained on us at the rate of two every minute, could be heard, and I might even say felt, coming from a great distance away, and it was not until after the terrific explosion (which shattered all the windows and shook the convent like a boat) that we knew that another had missed its mark. The suspense eventually became so great that we decided that we must get away somehow, and a shell crashing through a part of the roof hastened this decision. We carried the wounded from the convent, down an open fire-swept piece of road, and through the still burning houses of the village.

We eventually reached safety, where we handed our wounded over to the ambulance, but it was well after daybreak before we reached our regiment. This experience so affected the doctor that the following day he had to be sent away to the base, and, as far as I am aware, has never been in a fit condition to return to the front.

After two days' rest we marched to Ypres, where we took part in the desperate fighting which took place towards the latter part of the year. I had the pleasure of seeing this beautiful old town with its famous Cathedral and Cloth Hall before it was much damaged by the Germans, and I also had a splendid view of the famous Cathedral of Rheims when passing through that place earlier in the war, a fact which I forgot to mention before.

During the time we were at Ypres I had a very narrow escape. I was struck by a bullet in the back of the head, which then splashed against a wall near by and was picked up at the time and given me by a friend who was walking just behind. Although I carried a souvenir as big as an egg on my head for several days, the swelling eventually went away all right, and I am now none the worse, except for a little scar which will always remain with me and remind me of that lucky escape.

[Sgt. Atwell, who has lost the whole of his bees while at the Front, wishes to restart on his return to civil life next month. Would anyone who has two healthy stocks to dispose of kindly send price and particulars to him at the following address? Headquarters, 1st Infantry Brigade, B.E.F., France.   Eds.]

March 2nd 1916

It was at the village of Zillebeke, just outside the town of Ypres, that I found the bee house to which I referred in my letter dated December 1st, 1914, and which appeared in the British Bee Journal dated 10th of the same month. At that time none of us thought the war was going to last so long, and the hope I expressed that the owner would soon be able to return to his bees I am now afraid will never be realised, for I expect by now that this little apiary has quite vanished.

Sgt. Atwell's Apiary

About this time - April - I noticed a number of dead bees outside the hives and a few crawlers. I sent a packet of dead bees to the British Bee Journal office, and the verdict was "Isle of Wight" disease.

However, I was determined to give the bees a chance, and so I put them all in clean disinfected hives and fed them up with sugar, using nothing in the way of medicine but 'Apicure', which I put in all the hives. There then came a marvellous change for the better; both complaints seemed to vanish, and I took during the season 500 lbs. of extracted and 205 sections, increasing the bees from five to fourteen vigorous stocks, which were all packed down on ten frames with a huge quantity of their own stores.

The ten frames were left because I was then away at the Front. They all but one stock came through the following winter all right, and when I was home for a few days' leave in February, 1915, they seemed to be in quite a normal condition. The majority of them started the spring well, and most of them were supered up and gave some honey. But both complaints now seemed to come back again in a much stronger form, and by the end of the summer (despite the disinfecting with Izal my wife gave them) they were all dead.

The disease seemed to vary with the weather, and some weeks my wife would write to say that she thought they were pulling round, and she had been able to super two or three more stocks. But a week or two later she would say how much worse they were, some of them only covering a few frames.

Of course, my wife did all that was in her power to pull them round, but she was not able to put them all in clean hives, or perform other operations which I should have been able to do, and so, of course, the honey take was very small. A number of the hives still remain closed up in the orchard, and when I go home this month (having completed my military service) I hope to make a short report on them. I also intend starting again with two hives, and perhaps some bee-keeper whom the new Act affects may be in a position to supply me with them.

Returning once more to my story. We find ourselves marching back for a rest and to re-organise after our great losses, which, after all, were nothing like so bad as those of the Germans, as, of course, they did all the attacking, and were mown down by our fire as they used to advance in such hordes in their endeavour to break through to Calais.

However, they never got through the thin line which at that time barred the way, and so I do not think they can have much hope of doing so now. It was at the end of November that we started our march back, passing through Dickebusch and Locre, then across the Belgian frontier into France.

We passed through the town of Bailleul, and on to a little village called Outtersteine. Here we billeted at the various houses and farms, and I was fortunate enough to stay at a farm the owner of which was a bee-keeper. His farm had been damaged by a shell; all his wine, eggs, and stores had been looted by the Germans as they were retiring back through the village, being pursued by the British.

However, this old bee-keeper never left his bees, and I hope to tell all about him in the next instalment of my story.

May 25th 1916

After our stay at Guttersteine had lasted some five or six weeks we received a very sudden order to move to a new part of the line. We started our march early in the evening, and reached the town of Merville about midnight, this place being about midway between Guttersteine and our destination.

We rested there for several hours until, daybreak, and then continued our march, which brought us in the afternoon to Bethune, quite a fair-sized town some ten miles from the firing line. Marching straight through here we made our way to the front, and launched an attack against the Germans at a small village called Festubert, at which place I had some very interesting experience in connection with the bees.

There was also a little hamlet called Gorre, which we passed through just before reaching Festubert, at which I found a quaint old cottage and bee garden, having some eight or ten skeps wintered down, and there was quite a lot of appliances and empty skeps in a barn, which proved that the people who once lived there had done considerable business with their bees.

We spent our Christmas at Festubert, and during our stay there, when things were a bit quiet, I would often take a walk to see the bees at the cottage. Unfortunately at each visit I would find one or two skeps less, sometimes caused by a shell droppings near, but in the majority of cases it was the Tommies (who were billeted in the cottage) trying to get at the honey.

At the last visit I made I found every skep gone. I was just beginning to think that my adventures with the bees around this part were finished, when one day a friend came running into the dressing station carrying two large frames of honey, which he told me he had taken from a hive at the other end of the village near the firing line. I learned from him that there were quite a lot of hives there, although many had been badly knocked about by shell fire.

Having nothing particular to do at the time I got him to take me up to the garden, although we ran some risk from shell and rifle fire. The house, which stood on one side of the main street, was quite near the old church, which was a total wreck. We passed through a small front garden and then through the house (which was badly knocked about, very little of the roof remaining) into the long garden, at the back of which stood the apiary of large frame hives running right down the side of the garden. But what a sight; I could do nothing for some moments but gaze - in silence on the scene before me.

Only about two of the dozen or more hives seemed to have escaped destruction from the murderous fire which only a few days before had been rained upon them. Huge holes made by shells of the heaviest calibre dotted the garden. Hives were torn to pieces, broken combs and frames scattered everywhere, and little clusters of bees, the majority of which were dead through exposure to the cold, made up a scene which I feel quite unable to properly describe.

Had the bees been suffering from any disease, such as "Isle of Wight" or foul brood, matters would not have been so bad, but a thorough examination which I gave them failed to disclose the slightest trace of anything wrong. They had plenty of stores, but I had some difficulty in finding combs containing honey which were not damaged much, but I managed to find a few which I tied together to take away.

Passing back through the house I found some postcards scattered about, and by the addresses on them I came to the conclusion that the owner of the apiary was Mons. Omer Francois. I also found some photos of the family, and have every reason to believe that one of the gentlemen must have been Mons. Omer Francois. I hope to tell later of a second visit which I paid to this apiary, also of one or two other interesting experiences which I had at this village.

August 31st 1916

The next time I paid a visit to the Apiary at Festubert I found that it was practically demolished; not only had many more shells fallen around, but most of the hives which were any good for the purpose were used to help make barricades or build up trench supports, as a trench now cuts right through the apiary. There was only one stock left, and there was no roof on the hive. The honey in the outside combs had granulated with the cold, but the bees were clustered in the centre, and upon examination I found several patches of brood in the middle.

This, if I remember rightly, was about the middle of March, and as I felt that the bees could exist very little longer where they were, I found the queen and sent her in a box to the British Bee Journal Office, but unfortunately she did not live long after arrival. There was so much wax lying about from the many broken combs that I decided to collect it, and melt it down. I therefore went a few days later and gathered it all up. I took it to an empty house a little distance away, where I found a big, round galvanised tank; this I half filled with water, lit a big fire under it, put all the combs into it, and boiled them well down, and then strained the contents through several thicknesses of very fine wire netting.

When this was cold I took a good sized cake of wax from the top of the water, which I re-melted into a more convenient size for carrying. I now have the cake of wax among my other curios, although, of course, it really needs refining again, as it is rather dark in colour, owing to its having been procured mostly from old brood combs.

The next place I should like to talk about is the Orphanage at the town of Bethune, some eight miles behind the firing line, but of course well within range of the Huns' big guns, and they frequently bombard the cross roads, railway station, and other important parts.

Once when we were resting at Bethune we were when we were resting at Bethune we were billeted at the Orphanage, as all the inmates had been sent to a safer part of the country. Only two or three of the staff remained to look after the small farm which included several stocks of bees. I soon got into conversation with them as I could see the bees wanted attention.

They were very pleased when I told them I understood the bees, as the man that usually looked after them was away at the war. Some section and shallow frame racks had been left on from the previous year, but they were badly fitted and wanted re-adjusting. This I soon accomplished, having to cut away several nice slabs of honey, which the bees were beginning to place in rather awkward positions through the racks not being properly fitted. In addition to the frame hives there was a bee house with several skeps full of bees, but I was unable to do very much to these as it was too early in the year. I paid several later visits to this apiary, and was always made very welcome by the people there.

November 30th 1916

Each time that we took our turn in the trenches, I usually managed to find a few moments to spare to visit some of the apiaries which I had previously found. But what a difference there was at each visit. The few remaining hives and skeps which had marvellously escaped the hurricane of shell-fire got less and less in number until there was scarcely one live bee to be seen in any of these deserted gardens.

However, a few weeks later, as the spring advanced, I was pleased to see quite a lot of our little friends busy on the trees and shrubs, which had somewhat escaped the fire of the Huns. Chief among these was the peach, with its lovely pink blossoms, with the gooseberry and currant following closely upon it. These bees, of course, had come from a safer part, back behind the firing line, where the shells had not reached them. It seemed strange to see these little insects busy gathering their stores with our own guns booming all round, and German shells bursting quite near, and which at any moment might burst in the very garden where they were so busy.

They seemed, however, to hum a note of defiance as they went steadily on with their work. Many combs were scattered about the gardens from the wrecked hives, but they did not attract many bees. It seemed as though they understood and respected this mass of wreckage - once a flourishing apiary. As I walked back through the skeleton of that which was once a house, I could not help thinking how lucky we bee-keepers really are here in England. Many of us have lost our stocks from "Isle of Wight" disease (I myself have lost the whole of mine), out we still have our hives and appliances for a fresh start, and, above all, we still have a roof over our heads.

In some of my early articles I told how I had endeavoured to fix up frame-hives and skeps which I had found knocked about, and how I hoped that the owners would soon be able to return to them. This was some time ago, but the war still goes on, and I cannot see how any apiaries within the fighting zone can exist at all now. Nothing can remain to mark the places where they once stood but a few scattered pieces of wood, once hives. However, the experiences I had among the bees at the Front during the early days of the war, I shall never forget, and I shall always treasure the many little relics that I was able to bring home with me, some of which I collected at considerable risk.

As I have now reached the end of my story, I can only hope that my efforts to describe my experiences have proved interesting to readers of the Journal. I hope to restart bee-keeping myself again next spring, and I have the consolation of knowing that whatever my misfortunes may be in the future, they can never touch those of the bee-keepers and the bees at the Front.

BEEKEEPING ON TWO FRONTS

PART TWO

NOTES FROM DERBYSHIRE
Don Wilson (Belper) and Tom Sleight (Clay Cross)

January 8th 1914

A short time ago, having rather more heather honey on my hands than I could well dispose of retail, I offered some to a fashionable grocer in a neighbouring town. When he saw my sample, and had tasted it, he pronounced it spurious, and asked all kinds of questions as to its origin, ending by offering me. 2s. per doz. less than I was asking. At the same time he showed me some "real Scottish heather honey, absolutely the best obtainable," which he was retailing at 1s. 8d. per lb. The appearance of this made me doubtful, so I took steps to obtain a sample 1/2lb jar. When I was able to taste and smell this sample, I was more than doubtful as to its origin. Some I sent on to the Editors, who pronounced it to be a "blend." My own opinion is that the amount of "heather" in it was very small.

I took steps to find out more about this honey. From the label on the jar I saw that it was put up by a firm of Scottish packers. Their wholesale list, which I managed to see, described it as a pure heather honey, quoted the price of 14s. 6d. per doz., and ended by saying that as the present heather season (1913) had been very short, orders must be placed quickly to avoid disappointment.

By the way, was not 1913 one of the best heather years on record? I consider that in this case the retailer was the victim of the wholesalers, who, at the least, were guilty of rather sharp practice. Now as to the sequel. I decided to offer my honey to a, rival firm. I took with me two samples, one being taken from the purchased 1/2lb. before mentioned. This I offered first, and was nearly thrown out of the shop as a cheat. I was told that anyone selling such honey as genuine heather ought to be prosecuted. When I offered my own they agreed to take it at my own price, which by the way, had risen 1s. a dozen, and would take all I could supply.

Of course, if I have any honey to offer at a future time it will go to the grocer who knows good honey, and is prepared to purchase an honest article at an honest price. British honey need fear no competition which is open and above board. Those who purchase the cheaper foreign article generally do so through ignorance, believing that all honeys are alike, but I have proved that when once they know the real thing they come again for more.

February 19th 1914

February 3rd was really a beautiful day. The bees were flying freely about noon, and I took the opportunity of the warm weather to take just a peep under the quilts of each stock. I may say that all my stocks were well fed up for the winter before the beginning of October, some with syrup and some with natural stores - heather honey chiefly.

What I found upon this first peep of the year induces me to pen these few lines, hoping they will be of benefit to fellow bee-keepers. I was really not very much surprised to find that most of my stocks were getting perilously near the top bar. The winter here has been so mild that there has been little inducement to the bees to cluster together.

Every now and again they have been able to take flight, and the result of such open weather has been a greater consumption of winter stores than usual. In my case, although my bees were not yet short of stores, I have judged it the wisest course to give each stock a cake of candy in order to be on the safe side. I am of opinion that during the next few weeks many stocks will die through starvation unless fed, and I would sound a note of warning. Do not be too sure that because your bees were well fed up for the winter they are safe now, but make assurance doubly sure | by giving them at once that cake of candy. The winter has not been normal, having been too mild, and mild winters mean lost stocks.

March 12th 1914

It is a hobby of mine to collect bee-books. Thus, when the other day a booklet entitled "A Worker on the Wing" was put into my hand, it was eventually placed on my bookshelf. When, however, I found time to examine it, I decided it must take its place among the unreliables of bee-literature. It is published by Messrs. Dawson and Watson, Ltd., of Manchester, and is one of a series of books intended for use in schools. It has evidently been written by someone who is no beekeeper, who possibly has never seen the interior of a hive, and who is certainly is totally unacquainted with present-day apiarian science. It sounds something like a twentieth-century repetition of the heresies of Huish.

Bees are made to carry on conversations in every-day English. This is, of course, an old trick but it is questionable whether it has not been worked to death by now.

I find that, starting with a swarm in May, another (presumably a maiden swarm) is thrown off at some later time, and that towards the end of the season, this maiden swarm is sufficiently advanced to allow of the owner taking out quite a large quantity of honey, and leaving enough for the needs of the bees during the coming winter. A most amusing part about it is that this swarm is led off by a virgin queen, leaving the old queen in the hive. Then the method of taking honey is one which I would not like to suggest should be incorporated in the next batch of "Hints for Novices." To quote verbatim: " Well, one wet day in autumn, when all the bees in the new hive were at home, they heard someone moving about outside, and presently some strong smelling smoke came into the hive. The bees did not like it, so they rushed to the door, but found the doorway stopped up with clay. A pipe was stuck through the clay and Mr. Brown was puffing in tobacco smoke to make the bees go to sleep."

Surely Mr. Brown's name ought to go down to history as one of the present-day leaders in apiculture.

This is how Mr. Brown hived a swarm: "He made sure at once that the young queen was amongst them, and then turned the hive over quickly on to the bench, so that the bees were underneath it. For a little while he kept the hole where the bees go in stopped up with grass, so that the bees could not get out before they had time to become used to their new home." Another extract might have been written more than a century ago. "The master of the garden in which we live calls it pollen. Out of this, too, some of the bees make the wax-boxes which are used to store our honey."

Shades of Huber! Wax made from pollen! This in the twentieth century!

The rest of the book is more or less on a level with the extracts already quoted. If children may not be taught something better than this, then leave Nature study alone in schools, at least so far as it refers to bees.

June 4th 1914

Up to the present I have not heard of many early swarms in this neighbourhood, but Derbyshire never is early in such matters so far as my experience goes. I have seen some exceptionally weak stocks this spring, and some on the other hand which have come through the winter well. Of my own I have had to super five to guard against swarming. I have never done this before at such an early date, and have visions of supers of honey from fruit blossoms. Bees have been working hard on plum and pear bloom, but now that apples are in flower the weather has chosen to change, and unless it becomes warmer my fruit blossom honey will remain visionary only. Usually my only surplus locally is from clover and the limes.

To-day (May 2) being rather finer than the past few days, I have made arrangements for commencing queen-rearing by splitting one of my strongest stocks and taking a few frames and the queen to an out-apiary. The de-queened portion will be tried with larvae in cups. Drones are now in the hives, so the time is quite opportune.

From time to time the question crops up as to the suitability of heather honey as a winter food for bees. I have before expressed my opinion that it is a good winter food. This season I have taken special notice, and I am able definitely to state that the stocks which went to the heather last August have wintered better with less consumption of stores, and have come through stronger in bees than those kept at home and fed up on syrup. As a consequence, they are now ready either for supering or dividing, whilst the others are having to receive special attention to get them ready for the clover-flow.

Perhaps if other bee-keepers would give their experience of heather stores during the past season we should go a long way towards settling the vexed question once and for all. I should like (if the Editor will allow) to add a note of personal thanks for the instructions given in recent numbers of 'B.B.J." for making an observatory hive.

Although I do not claim quite to come under the head of 'Novices,' I found the article most helpful, and was waiting each time for the next contribution. I am not a "Croesus," and so have never been able to afford an observatory hive before, having always had something else to do with my money. But now, with the Editor's help, the expenditure of a few shillings, a little labour, and a little ingenuity, I am set up for a time. My hive is only made of deal, enamelled white, but next winter I intend to make another in mahogany.

June 18th 1914

"Tis not in mortals to command success,
But we'll do mere—deserve it."

May one who until lately was a comparative novice at that annual event known amongst some bee-keepers as "going to the heather" venture upon a few words of advice to those who may be, like he himself was a few years ago, anxious to go, but lacking knowledge and experience of the best ways of carrying out the operation. It may sound somewhat of a paradox to say that "success at the heather" is not gained there, but in the more prosaic apiary at home.

Like other achievements which are at all desirable, it must be prepared for months in advance. It is not a mere matter of taking bees to the moors, placing them in the most favourable, situation, and then trusting to luck. We learn from our successes; possibly we learn more from our failures. What I here wish to teach is the result, as much of failure as of success. Most bee-keepers have had one harvest of honey before the time arrives for the annual migration to the heather. Although perhaps the most glorious event in the bee-keeper's calendar it is not to be entered upon lightly and without due consideration. Success may come even to the foolish, but the experiment is most likely to end in dire and dismal failure.

Remember that from early spring you have been working your stocks to their utmost extent, stimulating the queen to the limit, and that now the harvest of lowland honey is over both queens and stocks are ready for a rest. But if heather honey is to be obtained no rest may be allowed. Strict necessity requires that any hive taken to the moors must be a mass of brood from back to front. For it is the quantity of brood taken, rather than the number of bees, that is to determine success or failure. How is this to be obtained? As soon as the clover flow is over, requeen at once.

This is not a treatise on requeening, or queen rearing, but by any method you can, see that a young queen is at the head of each stock, and by gentle stimulation if necessary make sure that she is laying to her fullest capacity. The presence of a young and vigorous queen puts new life into the stock as well as assuring combs solid with brood.

This, then, is the first essential, and must be thought out not the night before the great event, but months in advance. Although moderately strong stocks may be taken with a view to obtaining winter food, it is only the very strongest that will give surplus at a time when the natural propensity of the bees is to reduce the brood nest and begin to cluster.

Perhaps next to having stocks fit to take, the chief essential is to have suitable hives to take them in. There are many hives on the market, all equally good for standing in the home apiary, but possessing all sorts of defects when it comes to travelling with them. The essentials of a good heather hive are that it shall be easily shut up ready for a journey, that when closed there shall be ample ventilation for bees so that combs do not break down with the heat, that it shall ride easily on a conveyance without any suspicion of top-heaviness, and that it shall pack easily along with others.

If then the reader desires to take his bees to the moors he must see that his hives possess these essential features. A hive for the moors ought not to stand on legs, for when loaded on a dray there make the hive top-heavy and cause a considerable amount of swinging. Instead of legs stout plinths about 4in. deep under the floor-board are all that is necessary.

The entrance should be such as can be closed in a minute with perforated zinc and yet will give the bees ample ventilation and perhaps more important still, it should run the whole length of the hive. Double-walled hives - that is hives with interior chambers loose, such as the 'WBC' although perhaps the best for home use, are difficult to pack securely, and should not be taken. All supers should be contained in the outer case; sections can be easily accommodated in the 'WBC" hanging frame, and the supers containing them will then be found to be interchangeable with supers of shallow bars. In packing, a piece of cheesecloth or coarse slacking may be laid over the brood chamber or even over the supers, and another super jammed down tight will hold all secure. Nails or screws through the plinths complete the packing. Combs should also receive attention.

Novices are regularly being warned to nail all frames and to wire all foundation. If this is necessary for the home apiary, it is doubly needful when it comes to transporting stocks. If this little piece of advice be neglected the would-be traveller will possibly find himself, as Pettigrew says, "A hive the poorer but a thought the richer." Have by a supply of drawn-out shallow bars, and if possible sections also, because, although bees will draw out foundation at the moors they seem to do it with reluctance, and much valuable time may be saved by having combs ready. These they will fill at times when they will not look at foundation.

Now as to transporting bees to the heather. Close all hives the night previous to the journey, and if possible travel during the night or early morning, so as to have the stocks on their new stands before the heat of the day. Even the method of transporting stocks needs careful consideration. I am of the opinion that a light motor-lorry is the best means, and intend to try it as soon as possible. Failing that, choose a four-wheeled spring dray. On no account take an ordinary two-wheeled vehicle.

Accidents happen to horses at times, and if the animal honoured by your choice to convey you and the bees to the moors chooses to lie down on the way. Well, a two-wheeler goes down with it, whilst a four-wheeler may be trusted to remain as a rule in stable equilibrium. Look well after the horse, and see that he is capable of doing his work in the time allotted for it, or, if prolonged rests have to be made on the road, the bees may suffer. I write from experience.

I once hired a horse which appeared to be splendid. He went well on the level, but when he came to the hills he refused to go, and no amount of persuasion could induce him to pull. He had to be taken out, and I had an up-hill journey of several miles to the moorland farm to get another. Result - a stock damaged (my best stock, by the way), my temper gone for the week. When I examined that horse I found he had sore shoulders. Such details as here pointed out make for success. Leave nothing except the weather to chance, and then if that is favourable you will be rewarded by a bumping harvest.

Pack your hives carefully on the dray; a few turns of rope will hold them secure, and then drive. If you have such faith in your packing that you need not look behind to see if bees are coming out, then so much the better.

On arriving, unpack the hives from the dray, place on their permanent stands, which may have to be of the makeshift variety, such as a few stones, and then, before loosing the bees, see that the horse is taken out of the field. Make everything secure; see that there is ample room for bees to work and that all is packed up warm. Success in the shape of good super's of honey may not come, but it pays me to take for winter stores only. One more thought - a queen excluder is scarcely necessary, as the brood nest is now contracting

July 16th 1914

On Friday evening, June 26th, I was called for to deal with a large swarm which had settled on the stump of a laburnum tree on the station embankment near here. It was eight o'clock, and someone else had already been trying to hive them, but without success. When I arrived, I found that the proposition was really very simple. If the skep were placed over the stump it was only a matter of time for the swarm to ascend into it. In such a public place it was not long before I had a crowd of spectators.

One lady with her little boy scaled the embankment to have a better view, and for her safety I lent her a veil. The conversation ran something like this:

"Is there a queen in the swarm? I should like to see one."

"Yes," I replied, "and if I see her I will show her to you."

A few minutes later the lady exclaimed, "Oh! there's a bee on my veil." I asked her to keep quiet and I would remove it. It was now nearly dusk, and with scarcely another glance, I took hold of this bee and tossed it into the air. Just as it left my fingers I recognised that it was the queen I had so served. I called to a friend who was by to keep an eye on the bee, and we saw it alight on the little boy's head. From there it was removed (carefully this time) and returned to the swarm, half of which was now in the skep.

This incident, Mr. Editor, would be discounted as impossible if it were included in an article of fiction, but it is the bare truth. I told the lady she must think herself highly honoured, that after expressing a desire to see the queen she should have been visited by the very bee she wished to see.

It was dark before the bees were quite in the skep, so I had to leave them, but fetched them next morning at four o'clock. They weighed 5lbs. and are now in my apiary and working well. I found afterwards that they probably belonged to a local doctor, and came to terms with him, which were mutually satisfactory

September 17th 1914

Since sending the article, in which I indicated that a motor might be preferable to a dray for moving bees to the heather, I have heard from a friend. In his communication he deprecated any attempt at moving bees by motor, having had one experience recently when all the brood was shaken and killed, by moving his bees a distance of forty miles. This made me pause to consider the question more fully, but after due consideration I decided to make one trial.

On August Bank Holiday Monday I moved eight stocks to the moors in a motor van. I never had such a quick removal before. From leaving home to getting back it only took four hours, inclusive of time taken in setting down stocks on their stands, making all secure, having breakfast and a look round the moor, the total distance being close on thirty-six miles by road, some of which was bad and steep. Nor did the bees or brood suffer in transit.

On the following day I took more by means of the old-fashioned dray. I am afraid that the Editors would hardly allow my comments on that journey to appear in print, so will not inflict them on your readers. Since then I have been several times to visit my bees. It is only this week (August 17th onwards) that the honey-flow has come on. On Thursday the bees were doing splendidly, and honey was being rapidly stored. I notice that when on the heather the alighting-board is always crowded with bees apparently doing nothing, whilst others are flying freely. Is this experience a purely personal one, or have other bee-keepers noted the same occurrence? My hive entrances are open full width. Given a continuance of good weather for a few days there should be a bumping crop. It will be extremely acceptable to me considering the price of sugar. Beekeepers should look to this latter item at once. Leave as much natural store as possible and take every stock to the moors if within reach. It will pay.

I have generally found a lull of a few weeks between clover and heather, allowing me opportunity to reorganise my stocks. I look upon queen-excluder at the best as a very regrettable necessity, and when on the moors have done better without it. Even if a young queen gives a certain impetus to brood rearing in a stock, by the time the bees are ready to come back from the moors there is little danger that there will be brood in supers.

November 5th 1914

Until recently I thought that I had exhausted all available ways of selling my honey locally, and I should have been prepared to affirm that everybody in the small town, which, for pecuniary reasons, I honour by my residence, knew where to obtain good honey at a reasonable price. The following will show that I was wrong and will perhaps suggest to others further ways of selling honey.

Towards the end of July an agricultural and horticultural show was held in the town. There was no honey class, but I offered to give a little display if I could be allowed to sell. The result, from my point of view, was a complete success. I succeeded in selling a very fair quantity of jars and sections, but better still, the advertisement was well worth all the trouble. First one customer and then another expressed the pleasure it gave them to know where pure honey could be obtained;

they bought some and have come again since. Consequently I am by now nearly sold out of summer honey, and that without troubling wholesale dealers at all.

The above may be a hint to others as to means of disposing of honey and getting the full value without having to sacrifice part of the profit to a dealer. With my heather honey I find that although some customers ask for and, in fact, prefer it, others have still to be educated to it, and it will take some time to gather round me a clientele of heather customers. I find that with regard to honey the ordinary economic principle of demand creating supply can be reversed. A supply properly put upon the market will create a demand which will in time exceed the supply.

For some time I have been revolving in my mind a project having for its end the production of a complete "Book of the Bee." Perhaps this is not the time for its production, but still that does not alter the fact of its necessity. If a few lines here will set other minds to work upon the same idea, they may in less troublous times bear fruit.

We all know to how many books we have to turn to obtain anything approaching a complete knowledge of all pertaining to apiculture. The "Book of the Bee," when produced, would be a complete encyclopaedia, of bee-lore. In this book special articles would be written by experts in particular branches of beework, and the total result would be a work unsurpassed in its completeness of detail, and up-to-datedness of its authorities. For example, the "History of Bee-keeping" would occupy one place, "Queen rearing" another, "Diseases" another, and "Bee Flowers" another. Dozens of other subjects present themselves after only a few minutes' reflection.

The book could be produced if a number of subscribers could be guaranteed in advance, or it might even be brought out in fortnightly numbers at about sixpence per number, when, doubtless, more purchasers could be found than by offering it as a complete volume at once.

April 29th 1915

Whenever the weather has been fine during the past week I have been engaged, in spring-cleaning my hives and changing the stocks. These stocks have come through the winter well, on heather stores only, and I am again confirmed in my opinion that heather honey is quite a suitable food for wintering on. For years I have never lost a stock by wintering on heather stores.

I have this year specially noticed the great consumption of stores that takes place in March when bees are busy breeding. A cursory examination of hives in February (the quilts were just lifted) showed quite a quantity of stores left for each stock. The spring-cleaning showed that, failing a natural source of supply very shortly; the bees will have to be fed.

The great change has all come in a months Bee-keepers will do well to pay attention to this point and not suppose that stores a month ago mean stores now. The season here is quite a fortnight later than it was last year, but so far as I have seen stocks are in good heart and ready to push on whenever the proper time comes. The best stock I have seen so far covered nine frames with bees, and had five of brood on April 10th.

In the same apiary a fortnight ago, foul brood was found in a stock purchased last year. I advised treatment with "Apicure." This was done, and now, without any other treatment, the stock seems to be absolutely cured. Not only is the young brood healthy, but the bees have cleared out all the diseased larvae.

I do hope that the editor will allow this to appear, and not suppress it in his modesty because it appears to take on the character of a testimonial.

A last word. Sugar is dear, but for all that do not let bees starve for lack of a pint or two of syrup given at the right time. The interest on the money thus spent will far outweigh anything that can be got by investing the money elsewhere.

May 20th 1915

Much has been written at various times about the wonders of the hive, and the owner of a few hives is, as a rule, never tired of entertaining his enquiring friends with tales of the birth of the queen, the industry of the workers, the life, work and death of a drone, and so on. But to me nothing is more wonderful than the spring revival in an apiary. I am always surprised when, after a hard winter, I once again hear the merry hum of my bees. Not that I would have you believe that I am a careless and indifferent beekeeper.

I pack up my bees well for winter, I see that they are well supplied with food, that the queens are all right, and the hives are weather and waterproof. But in so doing I have a feeling that I am assisting at the last rites of a friend. For me there will no longer be the sight of the heavily laden worker returning with her load of pollen, the shrill note of the drone will no more be heard, the flash of wings in the sunshine will not be seen again, until spring returns; and spring is then so far away.

A visit to my apiary in the depth of winter is like visiting a city of the dead. It needs a strong imagination to picture that behind those wooden walls life is still in existence, only awaiting the call of spring, the first snowdrops and crocuses and a balmy day. I know it is so, and yet I am always surprised when, on visiting the hives on some fine day in early spring, I once again see outward signs of life. The winter-packing of my bees was to me a funeral; the spring revival is a great and glorious resurrection. Am I less hopeful than the bee-colony? I have the experience of years to guide me in my knowledge that a resurrection will come.

Not a bee in any of the hives, unless it be a queen, has ever experienced before the cold of winter daily becoming more intense until it finally compels them to form that dense cluster in the interior of their hive. Whence comes to them that spark of hope, causing them to hold so tightly to life, and ere the winter be half gone to commence once again the labours for the coming summer, which none perhaps will see?

We may ask in vain whether it lies in the interior consciousness of individual bees or whether in that communal consciousness which Maeterlinck calls the "spirit of the hive." Certain it is that no individual bee has the memory of such a previous time. In the hive there is nothing similar to Tennyson's "Many wintered crow that calls the clanging rookery home."

There is here a lesson to the individual bee-keeper, and to the world at large. It need not be pointed out. He who will may read it and learn it. Once learned, surely it will influence one's whole life. And when spring has once again revived the dormant life of the hive, what then?

June 17th 1915

I speak from memory only, not having made notes from year to year for my future guidance, but I cannot remember during the last fifteen years, a season which appeared so backward at the beginning of May as did the present season.

My bees certainly seemed to be at least a fortnight behind their usual time. Since then great changes have come upon the scene, and I can write that never have my bees been so forward as they were at the beginning of June. Ordinarily, the May honey flow in my district is merely enough to give a gentle stimulation to the bees in preparation for the flow from the clover in June.

This year not only has it stimulated the bees to breed, but has sent them well into supers, so that for the first time I have been able to take off honey before the end of May. From appearance, taste, and my knowledge of surrounding crops, I judge that this honey is mainly from sycamore, in which bees are still working, although the crop is rapidly passing away.

Trees of this variety vary greatly in their flowering periods. Some were in full bloom before apple blossom could be seen, others, long after apple blossom has disappeared, are just in their full glory, whilst the earlier ones have long been in seed. Even where not present in quantities great enough to ensure a surplus of honey in the supers, they help considerably to bridge the gulf of time between fruit bloom and clover, and for that reason alone I look upon them as one of the best bee flowers.

Now (June 13th) I see that white clover is making its appearance along the dry patches by the road-side, so that I expect in a week we shall have the main honey flow upon us. But the weather is terribly dry, and a good soaking of rain is required to ensure that to which we are all looking forward - a good flow from the clover.

Swarms have been pretty numerous and of good size. All round the district I can hear of them; some have been successfully hived by their owners; others have disappeared only perhaps to turn up in another district to enrich someone, who, having lost all his bees, has left his hives open to attract stray swarms. I have seen such cases, and have heard of others on unimpeachable authority.

Oh ! for that Diseases Bill to make such a proceeding a crime. A man who, in these times of "Isle of Wight" disease can leave his infected hives open, not only does not deserve a swarm but deserves a heavy fine for his questionable behaviour. He injures his neighbours in a double sense. He robs them of their swarms, and causes their bees to become infected by disease germs.

I have seen the ravages of "Isle of Wight" disease in this county during the last few weeks. In some cases one is inclined to say, "Serves him right; he never ought to have bees." I refer to those people - I do not call them beekeepers - who wait for the expert to put on supers and to take them off, whose hives are covered with the cast-off clothing of the last ten years or more, who take all they can from their bees and give nothing back, and then begrudge a small subscription to the local association. They are totally ignorant of the least knowledge of bee-life, and are a danger and a menace to all good beekeepers. It may be a drastic proceeding to advocate, but such keepers of bees should be suppressed by law.

There are others, often merely workingmen, who have invested their hardly-saved shillings in bees and have been obtaining good interest upon them whilst gradually gathering together a small apiary. Their bees also, in spite of the greatest care and cleanliness, have gone under. One such bee-keeper said to me, "It is not the money loss I bother about so much, although that is nearly twenty pounds, but I cannot bear to think that my bees, which worked so hard for me last summer, should have gone during the winter and spring. Has it been my fault; is there anything more I could have done?"

Such bee-keepers will rise superior to misfortune given time enough but I am afraid the "old guard" will never again see the bee garden full of hives. It is a tragedy - a tragedy of millions - and it might have been well in hand years ago.

July 22nd 1915

Congratulations first of all to our local exhibitor, Mr. Pearman, who, by his success in winning the gold medal at "The Royal," has not only brought honour to himself but has successfully demonstrated, not for the first time, the superlative excellence of Derbyshire honey.

When last I contributed a few notes I was congratulating myself upon the exceptionally early season and the good prospects of a record honey harvest. I am sorry to say that these prospects have not matured into realities. The very warm weather of early June burnt up all the ground crops and dried up the ground so that very little clover could show itself.

When rain came the weather never again picked up, and very little honey has since been gathered. In fact, I have had to feed nuclei to prevent total starvation, and that with plenty of clover in the fields and limes coming into bloom. There may still be a. short flow of honey if the weather will only mend, but I am afraid that any gathered now will be tainted with honey another record harvest.

Of course, I may be disappointed; I am almost certain to be disappointed; it is ever so. But that lessens none the less the joys of anticipation. It will not be my fault if that harvest is not a success. Once again I will set out what I consider to be the essentials to such a success.

First see that none but strong stocks, full of bees and brood are taken, and that there is a vigorous young queen at the head of each stock. If, when the time for the heather comes, stocks are not in that condition they must be made up to it. Secondly, see to it that the supers, whether sections or shallow bars, contain drawn-out comb; bees will store in them when they will not look at foundation.

Be certain that all hives shut up securely and stack easily on the dray, and, if you are not an expert horseman look after the bees yourself, but leave the horsemanship to a properly qualified carter. The latter point makes for ease and peace of mind. If it happens to be your first journey to the moors you will find that you know much more about bees and bee-keeping after the journey than you did before.

Like "Dartmooriensis" I also noticed the editorial reply to the query on 'unsealed brood.' I came across a similar case in my little bit of expert work this spring. There was no wax moth in the dew. In spite of frequent and copious washings of rain the excrement of aphids is still thick upon the leaves of limes, beeches, and oaks, and that is almost sure to mean "tainted honey."

But "Hope," the poet tells us, "springs eternal in the human breast," and now my thoughts turn towards the heather, and I am already revelling in anticipation of an hive, nor had it been over drugged. I diagnosed it as a form of foul-brood, and judged that 'Apicure' would be a good thing. This was tried and a cure resulted. This point now arises, "Are we to be troubled with another disease?" Perhaps other more capable and experienced bee-keepers have also seen this phenomenon, and will report upon it.

One more thought. Mr. Smallwood speaks of the varying temper of bees. This is often inexplicable, I never knew bees worse than they were in July, 1914, during the hot weather. Ordinarily my bees are quite mild, and I can handle them with, little or no protection, but at that time I began to think that to be a bee-keeper one would have to invest in a suit of plate armour. They quietened down again just as remarkably later on.

On inquiry I found that most bee-keepers in this district had the same experience at that time. Hybrid stocks were unapproachable. Whilst just looking into the supers of such a stock for a friend I was assailed by the bees with such fury that I had to beat a retreat, and acknowledge for that time, at least, an ignominious defeat. I have often had bees crawl up my legs when they have first settled on my boots, but these were more than crawlers. They flew, as though they knew the way under the bottom of my nether garments, and I had quite a busy time later picking out stings from the calves of my legs.

September 22nd 1915

The heather is out, and so commences the most glorious time in the bee-keeper's year. Some compensation is surely needed here, for since the end of May there has been little bee-keeping weather. My stocks have been kept tremendously strong all the summer, and have only needed a few weeks' fine weather to render a good account of themselves, but this has been denied. Local records say that July was the wettest month ever known in Derbyshire. What wonder, then, that no honey came in, and that nuclei have had to be fed! This also accounts for the heather being so late.

In fact, on Saturday, August 21st, there was not a sign of heather honey in my hives. A week later I found it necessary to rearrange some stocks, and to give more room after less than a week of honey flow. Those whose experience of bee-keeping has been limited to the gathering of low-land honey do not know the full joys of their craft. A visit to the moors on a warm day in August, when the bees are working as they never seem to work elsewhere, is to experience the greatest joy a bee-keeper can know. His stocks are at hurricane strength and packed into the smallest possible compass in the simplest of frame hives, and the honey seems simply to be pouring in.

Let him stand between the hives and the heather and hear the sweet music of the bees' hum as they wing their flight to and fro. There they go, just overhead, a never-ending procession, each bee intent solely on one work - the gathering of the last drop of nectar before winter sets in. when no, more is to be gathered. The flight of each bee is like the twang of a bow-string, the cumulative effect like the resonance of a thousand telegraph wires on a winter's morning. On such a day veil, smoker, and carbolic cloth may all be dispensed with. The bees do not seem to resent interference in the least. The whole hive may be turned inside out, and they will still continue their work.

Would you know the real taste of heather honey? Then take some warm from the hive and eat it on the spot. No honey, no sweet in all the world, was ever half so delicious. When it has been pressed from the comb at home and is cold it seems somehow to have lost the best of its aroma and flavour. Perhaps the environment has much to do with it, and the bee-keeper is in the proper frame of mind when surrounded by his bees to appreciate a real sweetmeat.

Take a walk on the moor among the heather. Not a soul is in sight over all its apparently limitless expanse. But the bee-keeper need not be lonely. All around him is the hum of a thousand insects - his own bees, wild bees, wasps, and hundreds of others which only a skilled entomologist could name. Dense clouds of white pollen rise from the open flowers at every step - a sure sign of a honey flow. Here and there a lizard darts across the path, only to be lost the next moment by reason of its excellent protective coloration; in the distance is heard the wild scream of the curlew, whilst nearer - almost from underfoot rise the grouse and fly off down the wind. This year at least they will have little cause to fear the sportsman's gun. Viewed from a distance the moor appears bleak, forbidding, and monotonous.

A closer acquaintance reveals an ever-changing panorama. Why, not even the heather is monotonous. This patch is a dark purple, the next much redder, some is almost white, whilst here and there may be found a rare specimen - a bit of pure white. I do not mean the product of the nurseryman's art, but the real white heather of Nature. Intermingled with all this are a few true heaths, the cross leaved, and the bell heather.

But beware that particularly inviting patch of bright green grass. It hides a bog, a bottomless pit perhaps, and if you tread there you will be lucky to escape with nothing more than a fright. Besides the patches of bracken relieving with their softer greens the dark peaty browns of the moor, and adding a freshness to the whole, here and there, under the shade of a rock, or in the gully cut by the moorland stream may be found the rarest and most beautiful of ferns. Let them stay in their natural habitat. Why despoil Nature for a momentary pleasure; too much vandalism has already taken place?

But, although the moor appears now to be deserted, there are not wanting signs of the time when it was a refuge for our forefathers. If you are lucky you may find a flint arrow head or stone hatchet; if you know where to look you will see the mounds of ancient earthworks or remains of stone circles where our ancestors used to worship.

Then back to the bees and the moorland farm, and if you are not satisfied with your ramble and ready for your bread and cheese and glass of milk there is something wrong with your aesthetic nature, and more wrong with your physical man.

January 6th 1916

The notes contributed by Mr. Macdonald in the Journal for December 9th mention a new kind of extractor. I believe that the first mention of this 'bilateral-multiple' extractor was made in the French journal L'Apiculteur for June and July.

Some months ago I took the trouble of translating the article into English, but have held it back until now, thinking that some more capable translator and critic would come along. I now send it with my comments made at the time. If the Editors are able at some future date to obtain the block illustrating the original article, the readers of the British Bee Journal will have a better idea of the extractor than words alone can give.

Much is claimed for the new machine, but I doubt whether practice would justify entirely all that its inventor says on its behalf. After twenty years of apicultural experience my father has just brought out a definite type of extractor capable, not only of emptying at once and the same time the two faces of combs of all the usual types, and that in a manner without reproach, but of extracting at one operation the honey of an entire apiary.

"The machine is composed of a barrel held upon a frame upon the arms of which rest the two extremities of the shaft, one of these extremities being furnished with a geared crank.

"On the shaft in the inside is fixed an arbitrary number of supporting devices, to each one of which four frames can be attached. The supporting device consists of arms of equal length having at their ends a stop, and at the hub a movable support which can

1. Slide so as to be adapted to suit every kind of frame;
2. Allow by means of a simple clip displacement the substitution of two half-frames for each frame;
3. Bend on a spring so as to seize and hold the frame like a big hand, like a large pair of automatic pincers, the grip of which is further increased by the rotation of the machine.

"The mode of operation is as follows:

'On lifting the cover, which is a kind of light hood, there is found in the mouth of the opening the arm which is to receive the uncapped frame. Each arm lifted in succession is held during the operation by a convenient brake. As soon as all the arms are fitted with frames (an operation performed in less time than with the older types of cages), the cover is shut and the machine rotated.

The honey, thrown out in the direction of the slant of the cells with easy rapidity, soon runs along the inner walls, and reaching the bottom of the barrel without remaining there flows out of its •own accord without the necessity of inclining the barrel.

From this short description one can predict what will be the scope of this unexpected invention for the bee-keeping industry. The amateur will no longer fear the grievous loss of time formerly demanded for the extraction of his honey.

The professional will no longer need to fear the risk of robbery caused by an operation which is never finished, nor will he need to encumber himself with a host of extractors, since with one only he will do the work in less time than with many of the ancient ones.

I give a brief outline of the decisive improvements guaranteed by the new extractor. The duration of the extracting operation is reduced beyond comparison, because the honey of twenty frames can be extracted in less than half the time previously taken for four. No more damaged combs, no pressure, no tendency to break down the thin intervening wall of wax. The brood is safe, because if the honey comes obliquely from the cells to run down the surface of the combs it is because it is liquid, and the larvae cannot follow the same path.

The selling price does not lose by comparison, because, put on the market at the same price as the four frame reversible extractor, the new extractor with have supporting devices does in the same time ten times the amount of work. The barrel can stand by the wall, avoiding in this manner the waste of room necessitated by the ordinary extractors, which take up much space in the workrooms, and sometimes cannot be passed through the doors.

In place of the noise formerly inseparable from extractors we have only a kind of a humming greatly resembling the noise of a swarm.

This enumeration of advantages so long desired might be much prolonged. Let it suffice me to add that the stability of this new extractor is perfect, both when in movement and at rest. Thus finishes the period when, in spite of fits of temper, we could not stop the dance of the barrel and the infernal racket of the cages and the gear.

"With economy of time, money, space, bees, wax, strength and trouble, what bee-keeper worthy of the name will pass by this indispensable harvester of honey? Rene Jacquet."

The bee-keeper may imagine at first, from the outline given above, that with the purchase of this new extractor, all the troubles of extraction will cease. Whether the machine will do the work claimed for it or not I do not know, but at least one criticism may easily be passed upon it.

The old style of extractor with which we have become familiarised, whatever be its faults, extracts evenly each side of the comb in turn. The new one above noticed, which claims to extract both sides at once, cannot, from the nature of its construction, extract the honey evenly. From the greater peripheral velocity the honey on the outer edges of the combs would be thrown out before that at the inner edges; thus we should have one part of a comb empty, whilst the nearer we got to the hub the more honey there would be left in the comb, and the greater the speed required to throw it out.

January 27th 1916

It is at the beginning of a new year that one can look back upon past experiences, draw lessons therefrom, and make plans for the forthcoming season. I know that the sentiment just expressed is as old as the hills, and has become to us very little more than mere cant. But still, I will venture to stick to it. Now, in the comparatively dead season, it is time to think on past, present and future.

If I were asked to state what is the lesson most forcibly impressed upon my mind by the experiences of the past year, my answer would have reference to the heather harvest. Last year's crop was late, short and sharp, and only in few places was a surplus obtained.

I have before time expressed the view that the ordinary hive is of little good for the moors. I am beginning to think it is almost useless. My best success last year came from a small hive, little more than a travelling-box, containing only eight standard frames and a super of shallow bars, into which the bees, for lack of room below, were forced to crowd. This hive had neither legs, alighting-board, nor porch, and I did not find that the bees were at all incommoded for lack of these luxuries. Such a hive takes up but little room when travelling, and is easily handled by one person. At least twenty could be packed on an ordinary dray without tiering up. I shall pursue the experiment further next year, I hope.

Like most others, bee-keepers will feel the pinch of these comparatively hard times. I wonder how many of our craft
were tempted to take the last ounce of honey from the hives last year, and then, because of the heavy price of sugar, neglected to see that their bees were well supplied with good syrup. My bees went into winter quarters on heather stores.

For years now I have found such honey good for wintering on. I hope again to have the same experience. But the winter so far has been quite mild and open, and again, as in all similar seasons, there will be great consumption of stores. Let us see to it that stocks are not unwittingly starved to death. Many stocks will already have begun to breed, and it is during breeding time that food is used up.

I question whether bee-keepers are now getting the proper equivalent in money values for their honey. All bee material has risen in price, glass bottles have been difficult to obtain, and are now nearly double in value, sugar for feeding is exceedingly dear, and yet I cannot see that honey is sold at any higher price than before the war began. For my own part I sell but little wholesale, but found that the grocers with whom I dealt were inclined to look upon honey as one of the first luxuries to be abandoned as unnecessary when the present trouble began. There is still a lamentable ignorance with regard to food values in certain quarters.

With regard to the bee-keepers' particular bête noire - microsporidiosis - I am really glad that up to now I can add little of value to the discussion, not having yet had the plague in my own apiary. I have seen plenty of it in various parts of the county, and have furthermore heard of its ravages in other apiaries. When it comes to me, if it does come, I intend not to go under without a fight. But there seems to be little to guide me, even in the experiences which bee-keepers have accumulated during this last ten years. Principally the records seem to be records of failure - not of success.

In conclusion, I may say that I am an optimist with regard to bee disease. The plague will die out, and I am inclined to think that when the storm has spent its force apiculture will be the hotter for the visitation. The stocks that weather the tempest will be those that are most vigorous. There will be a survival of the fittest from which the bee-keeper can again extend, being sure that he has hotter bees than ever he had before.

September 21st 1916 (Tom Sleight)

I have just come in from a ramble on the moors, but where are the bees? I went to a part of the moors where three years ago I found a lot of hives by following the bees in flight.

To-day I spent three-quarters of an hour close to where those hives were, a lovely afternoon. Heather beautifully in bloom (but not such a purple mass as three years ago, and does not look like being), and, by the way, Tommy humble bee was at work on it. It must be fairly laden with honey, for there were hundreds of them, but I had nearly given up in despair of seeing a hive bee on that part of the moor when - what was that?

I can tell the hum of a hive bee in a tick. I bent down, and there was one solitary bee, its wings very badly chafed and worn. I wondered if it would be able to reach home with its load, for there was not a doubt it would be about a mile from home.

Where I have seen about twenty hives there was not one on that side of the moor. On the other side where I have seen nearly thirty there are five, and four of those were only taken up last Wednesday, but two of them had half-filled a super, and although it was a cool, windy day they were working for all they knew.

I had been wondering all the afternoon how it was Mr. Don Wilson had no bees there, but when I got back home I picked an old 'Record' up someone had sent me, when the first thing I dropped my eyes on was, Sapper D. Wilson, so it is the war again as well as "Isle of Wight" disease that is keeping bees from heather.

I think about all bee men from Clay Cross side lost all their bees last winter, I can only find one place where bees have done well, and they had three stocks which have swarmed and swarmed again – they actually had a top swarm on August 10th. I could only wish I had it on yon moors now with a rack of sections over it. I took a small driven lot to the moors on August 10th, and heather was well out then. I saw five bees at work on it then I call that very early.

I have not had any bees for two years, till about July 16th someone sent me a small cast of "Goldens," and they seem as though they mean living. They hived themselves in an old empty hive. I saw a golden bee flying about these old hives two or three days before they came, but I never dreamt any bees would come. How Nature has been trying to populate all empty hives!

I know of three distinct places that have had bees come in July. Well, I put a bottle of food on mine, and they are doing well. That started the old bee fever again, and I had to go and buy another swarm, but they had been hived on foundation which had all dropped down. All the combs were as one, there was no parting them without breaking, so I got them on to six frames in a box and took them to the moors. They will get a bit there; they will do to join up to the others.

The cold wet June and early July caused clover to be very late round this part, but I never saw more; field after field a white mass of it. Those few who had any bees have had some full supers this year, at a time when other years the flow would have been over.

January 31st 1918 (Tom Sleight)

There has been a lot of very interesting news in the B.B.J. this last few weeks from different writers. So I am just going to try to fill up a little blank space with a few things I have noticed in the bee line since last March. About that time I had cause to be working near Dover for a few weeks, and as I travelled about I was taking particular notice as to the number of bees round there. I saw very few, but plenty of empty hives. I might have gone by some and not seen them, but on one road from Barham to Sandwich, 10 or 11 miles, I passed one hive in Nonington and one near Eastry Church.

What a weight of honey must have vanished into thin air from off all those pieces of good clover and sainfoin I saw around there! I have often wondered this summer how those two hives have gone on.

One other thing I forgot to mention. I should certainly have liked to have seen Ripple Court - the name so well known to all. readers as the home of Mr. Sladen and his "Golden" bees. I was coming from Deal through Northbourne one night when I saw the name, " Ripple Court - two miles," on a guide-post; and that was as near as I got.

The bees certainly don't have to fly over many hedges in that part; it is like going over Beeley Moors, crossing some of those fields, and if there was one place more than another where I would liked to have planted a dozen bee-hives, it was on that roadside from Northbourne to Betteshanger.

Well, to come back to Derbyshire, which I did the last Saturday in April, to find one of my two hives very bad with the "Isle of Wight" disease. I set to work and sprayed it with Dioxogen, and in a week I did it again; after that I saw very few bees crawling, and, the weather being superb, they seemed to be making fair headway, although they were reduced to a double handful. Note, this hive had stood by itself all winter; the bees were a cross, more yellow than black, and the finest queen I ever saw.

Well, at this time I had to bring my hive of "Goldens," which was a couple of miles away, and stand by the side of No. 1. Bad policy, some would say, seeing it was free from disease. I did not think one could give some bees "Isle of Wight" disease, try as one might, but one can - as I have found out since.

It was a fairly strong lot, and they seemed to take to the change all right, but they did just what I expected they would do the first cool day that came - they set on to rob No. 1 out, it being a weak lot.

I was potato-planting at the front of the hive, and I saw them start. As I had no carbolic acid handy, I fastened No. 1 up, so the bees could not get in or out. I kept them fastened up two days; then, as it had turned warm, I let them out again, and they did not bother that day. The next day it was hot, and when I went to look at them they were at it again. I thought, " Well, you will get 'Isle of Wight' disease now, as you have been stealing that honey," and they had killed about all the bees in No. 1. The queen was wandering disconsolately about the comb; for a good job they had not killed her.

If anyone had come up just then I would have given them that queen as useless to me, but nobody was near, so I did the next best thing. I exchanged hives, and gave No. 1 all the flying bees from the "Goldens"; that gave the queen enough bees to cover three frames of comb, and there were 10 lbs. of honey left in the hive. She was three days before they took to her to make her lay: then she set to with a will to turn those 10 lbs. of honey into bees. It was like putting a small swarm to her.

Of course, I sprayed them both after that lot, and for six weeks I never saw a. crawler. Although the "Goldens" had five frames of comb full of brood when I exchanged them, No. 1 hive was full up on eleven combs first. It has not been my lot to see such combs of brood full from top to bottom bar, and from end to end, with only about an inch of honey in the corners, for some time.

As it was getting into July, I could not expect much honey from clover. I thought, "What a stock to take to the heather," but now "Isle of Wight" disease showed signs of coming again, so I took the combs out to spray them one by one, when, to my horror, I found foul brood had set in very badly; in fact, I never saw it worse. It seemed to all come in a fortnight. I thought if Dioxogen would cure "Isle of Wight" disease, I would try it on foul brood; so I sprayed it all among the brood and eggs. Honey was coming in from the clover, so I put the super on, and they got about 15 lbs.

The super had been on ten days, when I took it off again, and took all the combs out of bottom of hive and sprayed them bees, brood, and eggs. That was the last week in July. I can't say at the moment what it has done for the foul brood, but I have not seen a crawler out of that hive since. Had the weather been anything like it was the last week in July they would have got 50 lbs. of heather honey, but as it is they have got from 15 to 20 lbs. in an eleven-frame super.

It was nearly all sealed over when I was up there on August 27th, with the super crowded with bees. To see that lot then anyone would hardly believe there were crawlers by hundreds outside the hive the last Sunday morning in April, and when I sprayed them the next day they seemed to come out for a cleansing flight, and they were about all crawlers in a few minutes.

Some writer says his were up flying again in two hours after spraying with Dioxogen. I am doubtful on that, for I sprayed the bees on the ground, but I think they were about all dead next day, so I turned the earth over them. T Sleight

February 14th 1918 (Tom Sleight)

Now, to turn back to the "Goldens". When I exchanged them during the robbing bout, they were a bit bothered to know which hive they belonged to, and which they were stealing honey from, but the next day, when I went to look how they were going on, No. 1 lot was working all serene and happy.

Not so the "Goldens," they were fighting and killing scores. I thought, "Oh, you are finishing those few flying bees from No. 1 hive off as they come home." As they had killed so many in the robbing bout, I left them to fight it out, thinking it would be over by next day, but I have since found out, to my sorrow, that when "Goldens" start fighting they never know when to stop.

I did not go to look at them for a few days, hut they were still fighting; they had killed hundreds, so I went back to the chemist's and got some carbolic acid, with which I painted the flight-board and front of hive.

I had to do it three times before they would stop; they were killing all the flying bees as they came in; they killed them till the outside combs of brood were chilled, after that, they seemed to settle down, and by the last week in July they had got full up on eleven frames of comb, and had a super full of bees; they are marvellously quick-breeding bees. I took them to the heather on the last Saturday in July, and thought what two grand lots I was taking - they looked like filling a super in no time.

But how soon one's hopes are dashed; they were there six days before they could get out of the hive for cold winds and wet days. The sun shone again at last, and out they came.

The heather was in full flow, but they had not been at work long before they found out that bees in strange places often hit the wrong hive when they come blustering in loaded, and they were not having any strangers, so they started fighting again. I could see any dark-coloured hybrid was soon walked out and slain, but they did not stop at them. If a yellow bee alighted about an inch above the entrance and then fell backwards, they pounced on it in a crack, and it was slain and marched off the flight-board.

I reckoned they were doing twenty every ten minutes, and as I had no carbolic acid with me I had to leave them at it; so it may be imagined what a heap there were when I went four days later. There were quite a capful, and all living honey gatherers that came in loaded. The peevish little demons I call them. I have seen, bees rob and fight where there has been no honey to get, but never in a big flow as it was coming in then.

It would be interesting to know if anyone else has ever had the same experience with "Golden" bees. I have taken the carbolic and painted front and entrance of hives. It gives them a chance to get in, as it clears all the fighters off the board, but they still keep killing odd ones. Scores were clustered on the flight-board all the while they were at the heather – a contrast to when they were working on clover. Some days, when I watched them, every bee was working its hardest, not a single bee scouting at the front. These "Goldens" have never shown the least sign of "Isle of Wight" disease that I have noticed; perhaps it is because I keep spraying them.

It is now Christmas Eve, and nearly four months since I penned the foregoing notes. Time and bees have altered so much in the interval that one lot of notes will perhaps jar with the other, but I think, at any rate, it will interest readers if I finish the yarn about those two stocks of bees. The weather was very showery all the time they were on the heather, and although they worked hard in the intervals, when I had left enough for winter I only had 20 lbs. of surplus for myself, but even then I certainly did better than our Scottish friends.

Well, the "Goldens," owing to their fighting so, what bit they stored in the super they would have wanted it to winter on had they kept all right, and they were strong the last week in September. They were crowded on eleven combs, and had at least one comb of brood to hatch out. As for the foul brood I mentioned, I could only find two cells with any sign, of it in them. I thought I had never seen such a strong stock put down to winter.

I had never seen a sign of "Isle of Wight" disease about that lot all the summer. Dioxogen had certainly kept the two stocks free from it, but to see them again a month after that it was as though a blight had come over those "Goldens" It was not lighting this time, for they were crawling about in thousands all over the garden The last time I was near the hive it was an inch thick in dead bees all round it.

If out of that good lot any survive the winter I will be greatly surprised. I don't think No. 1 lot had got it so bad; in fact, I saw few crawlers about that hive till just before Christmas, then I saw a few.

March 14th 1918 (Tom Sleight)

I would here like to say a few words on the merits, and demerits, of Dioxogen. I used it on No. 1 hive from October, 1916, to October, 1917, and, so far as I could see, with good result, for the stock covered eleven combs in October, and I believe it will winter. I used it more or less the same on the "Goldens," and they appear to be disappearing fast. I bought an 8-lb. swarm on July 1st, and in three weeks they had got "Isle of Wight" disease bad. I sprayed them with Dioxogen times many, but they kept dwindling away till there were scarcely enough to cover two combs - it never seemed to do them a bit of good.

In the meantime, Mr. Smith, of Cambridge, had sent me a sample of Flavine, and I had it a month or so before I thought of using it. As Dioxogen had done my other two so much good, I wanted to give it a fair trial on this swarm, and I run it on rather late before I used the Flavine. But, anyway, I could see that swarm was vanishing fast, fresh crawlers every day, till they only covered two combs, and I decided to give Flavine a trial. Well, I got them sprayed three times before the cold weather came on, and whether Flavine is any good or not, I have only seen about a dozen crawlers outside that hive since. If they live the winter through they will be a marvel, as they got so weak.

If Flavine is going to make combs and hives so that bees can work and live in them after having "Isle of Wight" disease, it will be a great boon. I for one am giving it a trial, but my firm opinion is that whatever combs, or sections, diseased bees have been on, it will be there years before they are safe to use for bees again.

The only things about the place that had been near my bees when they died out three years ago were an observatory hive with one frame, and a section rack with twenty-one worked sections in for heather honey, and I put three of these worked-out sections on this swarm with the result that they had " Isle of Wight " disease in three weeks. The frame out of the observatory I put in No.1 in September, 1916, with the result that they started with the disease in five weeks. Certainly, I never disinfected any of them before I put them on. I simply wanted to see how things did work; they had Naphthalene in with them in the boxes, but that does not appear to hinder it - one had better burn the lot.

I should just like to give my impressions of the "Golden" bees. I believe they are a good bee to make big stocks, and stand in one place all the time, but they are no good to move about, and, unfortunately, I had to move mine twice this year. It seems to start them fighting. Could they have stayed where they were at first they would have given a good account of themselves, for there were no more bees within two miles of them. Now, a few remarks as to the season. 1917 will rank as one of the best years for bees round here that I ever knew.

One flower followed another in quick succession, with never more than a day or two of hindering weather at a time. Bees built up quickly, swarms were fairly plentiful, and June swarms gave from 50 to 60 lbs. of surplus honey. There are not many bee-keepers round here now, but each one lost a swarm during the season. One young man I know had two come out within five minutes of each other, and they took off together.

We spent some time looking for those bees as they were part "Goldens" he was sorry to lose them. 1 always thought we should hear some time where they got to, and I came across them in one of my rambles in November, five miles, as the bee flies, from where they started. This bee-man said, "I did have a grand swarm of part "Goldens" come in July." I said, "If you can tell me about the date they came, I can perhaps tell you where they came from", and it proved to be correct. There were only about thirteen hives taken to the heather this time; and it was earlier than I have ever known it. Honey was coming in by July 21st. I saw 'Tommy Humble' working on it then. I took my bees the week following, but I missed the best week, and I never saw more bloom on it. Lot us hope for another good year in 1918.

February 2nd - It will be only fair to your readers if I just give a brief account of the end of those bees. They were half a mile away in am allotment garden, and a fortnight ago to-day I found them all dead, they looked as if they had been dead a month or more.

Now, I was not surprised to find the swarm, and the "Goldens" dead, that does not speak very well for the Flavines, as I had sprayed the swarm three times with it, and the "Goldens" once, still, I should not condemn it, as it was getting into October before I used it. Perhaps someone who has used it more in the middle of the summer will say how their bees have wintered after it; but the No. 1 lot beat me, dying out like that. I never saw a sign of any crawlers outside that hive till the latter end of November, and then not many. Then to go and find them all dead, with 15 to 20 lbs. of honey, and a great lot of bees, makes one wonder, after colonies with half that quantity of bees had gone through the winter we had last year, does it take a whole year to clear some stocks out after they commence with "Isle of Wight" disease?

Dioxogen does not seem to really cure them, unless it is that one keeps re-infecting them by giving them comb or putting a bee escape on. It might easily be done like that. There were a few dirty marks on the combs, but the bees are all diy, quite different from the swarm, they, when I tried to brush them off the combs, were all rotten together.

I was at Carlton, near Worksop, last week end, and two new beginners had lost all their bees quite in a similar manner to mine, and two more old beekeepers near

Chesterfield have lost all their bees this autumn in the same way, so the disease is very rampant around us yet.

October 10th 1918

Bees in France. How very much I should have liked to head this little article with the old title of " Derbyshire Notes." But, alas! For more than two years I have been separated from my bees, only seeing them at the rarest intervals. The causes are the war, and the service I have been, and am, rendering to King and Country. Much of this service has taken place in Ireland, where, I am sorry to say, what few bees I was able to find were kept in the most wretched state that it is possible to imagine. I must not, however, conclude that this is the general Irish system. The district I was serving in was backward in many other respects besides in apiculture.

But to leave that. I am now in France, and have been there for some time. Of course, I have kept a look-out for bees and bee-keepers wherever I have been and I have moved about considerably. At times I have caught passing glimpses of apiaries as I have rushed along the main roads of this beautiful country, either in a heavy lumbering motor-lorry or in one of Mr. Henry Ford's automobiles (sometimes). But only three times have I been able to get into intimate touch with a French apiarist.

Here, as everywhere else, the war casts its shadow, and in talking to the beekeepers I have found that the one who was specially interested in 'les mouches' was away at the war, so any conclusions I may arrive at may not be entirely just. It seems to me, though, that our gentle cult is in a backward state here. Only once, when rushing by on a car, have I seen an apiary of frame hives. The apiaries I have visited have been composed of skeps or box-hives. The honey is still taken from the bees by the cruel ancient method of suffocating them at the end of the season. Modern methods seem to have been heard of, but initiative is lacking to put them into practice. It has interested me to find that the same superstitions as exist in rural districts of dear old England exist here.

For instance, if a member of a family dies, the bees must be informed of the circumstance, and a piece of crepe must be tied to the hive. Memories of happy times spent wandering amongst bees and bee-keepers at home came back to me vividly when once again I heard these quaint old ideas set forth with so many authentic instances to back them up.

It will be seen that up to the present I have not had the good fortune to find a truly up-to-date and enlightened beekeeper, although I hope to do so. I know that such do exist in profusion and that apicultural societies are doing good work in educating bee-keepers and spreading a knowledge of scientific apiculture. But by reason of war, I have been tied to beaten tracks and strictly limited in my searches, and therefore I do not wonder that I have not found them.

I should not call the part of France that I have seen a really good bee country. It is too highly cultivated wheat, oats, rye, barley and sugar-beet seem to be the chief crops. Of course, there are patches of clover, lucerne, sainfoin and buckwheat, but these do not make up for our good old English hedges, meadows and pastures. Such do not exist here. I should think that hives which are strong in early spring would pick up a fair harvest from fruit bloom, for many cider-apple trees are to be found everywhere. I am afraid that the one little English pronoun "I" appears more often in this article than any other word. As it is more of a personal narrative than anything else, I ask for indulgence. My thoughts fly forward to the time when once again I shall be at home with wife and children, with bees in the apiary and my bee-books close at hand, when peace shall once more reign on the earth, and when instead of beating my sword Into a ploughshare I'll be able to make of my bayonet a tolerably efficient uncapping knife. Till then I can only live in the memory of apicultural delights. To assist this memory, to make it more vivid and the pictures it calls up more real, now let me turn to Maeterlinck's "La Vie des Abeilles " which accompanies me "partout."

September 4th 1919

It is now nearly three years since I had the pleasure of contributing anything to the "B.B.J." with the exception of a short article written from France last year. The cause has not been lack of interest, but simply lack of suitable matter. Life in the Army does not lend, itself to expressions of opinion on the current state of apiculture. Now I am back, but on return find that my three years' service has cost me dear. Out of a splendid apiary of twenty-four stocks not one remained on my return! The prevalent "I.O.W." disease and a certain amount of unavoidable neglect are responsible for the loss. Had I been at home - but then it is no use thinking what might have been. Possibly my presence would not have affected the ultimate result one little bit. But I do think that in cases such as mine something should be done by way of Government grant to make it easy for the bee-keeper to start once again on his hobby. As it is, we, who have done our little bit in the army, find on our return that the cost of re-starting an apiary is to fall entirely on our own shoulders.

The other day I applied at the Post Office for a form on which to claim from the Civil Liabilities Fund. The questions are so numerous and so intricate that no bee-keeper who merely kept his bees as a hobby can possibly answer them. I know at least that I cannot do so, and so I am reluctantly compelled to pass over that idea.

However, I have been able to make another start on my own, and now have six stocks of various sorts, with which, I hope, to re-establish my fallen fortunes. They are now on the heather, where I hope they will store enough honey to see them through the winter, and possibly give a little bit for sale. In past years I have often written a little on going to the moors. My experiences have been many and varied, but all have contributed more or less to my education, and now I think that I have reduced the problem of transporting bees to the moors to something like workable proportions. I remember that the first time I attempted the journey was with a pony and dray. It was something like five hours on the way, and met with many and varied adventures.

This year I was unpacking my stocks in less than an hour from leaving my own apiary. The secret of it all is motor transport. I used a Ford motor, with a grocer's delivery van body. The cost was little more than I should have had to pay for horse transport, and the gain in time, and ease, and security could not be estimated.

The hives I have taken to the moors this year are those in which my bees have passed the summer with me, 'four being frame hives, (and two being the old fashioned skeps). This has simply been caused by lack of time to prepare more suitable moor equipment, but next season I hope to have special heather hives ready. For years I have been experimenting for the purpose of finding what is a suitable hive. I believe that I found it in 1915, but have not again been able to try it. The hive is not an evolution of the frame hive into a complicated structure, but is a simplification. It only holds eight standard frames in the body, and has a super of eight shallow frames. There is neither porch nor alighting board, nor legs. In fact, it is the simplest form of frame hive that can be made.

On the moors, a few stones take the place of legs, or a few wooden blocks are carried separately for the purpose. The roof is shallow, and nearly flat, sloping slightly to the rear. Quite a large number of hives of this kind can be carried in a motor van. Of course, such a structure is entirely unsuitable for work in the home apiary being far too restricted, but it can be used during the summer for rearing nuclei.

When August draws near, and the time comes for moving to the moors, the stocks in the large hives can each be transferred to the special heather hive. Note that if it be a ten-frame stock to be transferred that there will be two frames to leave at home. These will be the two outside ones, of course, and at that time will not be likely to contain brood. If the eight taken are all full of brood, so much the better, for to a great extent it is the brood taken that decides the return of heather honey. Put on the eight shallow frames for a super. The restricted brood nest will cause the bees to be crowded into this super. Thus there is no question of the bees refusing to enter a super, they are already there. Of course, in transporting hives so packed with bees, ample ventilation must be provided.

Later - I made a visit the other day to see how things were going on the heather. A few fine days had elapsed since the arrival of the bees, and I found that they had been doing well. The skeps had increased greatly in weight, and the only frame hive supered had quite a lot of honey already gathered. I had the joy of tasting the most delicious sweet on earth - heather honey-comb taken warm out of the hive, and eaten on the spot. Those who have never tasted this do not really know what honey is.

Since then we have had a succession of dull, cold, wet days, and I fear little more has been done. I can only hope for a few more bright days to lengthen out this harvest. The moorland farmer tells me that, owing to the drought early in the year, he does not think that the heather will last long.

Since coming home I have seen nothing of my old friend, Mr. Tom Sleight. I'll warrant this short article sets him writing somewhere.

Now for one more remark before finishing, I have known the "B.B.J." for many years, and have always appreciated its contents. I am so glad to find on my return, whilst looking through accumulations of the paper, that it keeps up its old standard of excellence. I hope that I am not casting any reflections on the issues of past years when I say that it appears to me to be better than ever. I hope that the Editors will not be too modest and refuse to print these last remarks.

[We thank Mr. Wilson for his kind appreciation. We are also very pleased, indeed, to hear he has been "demobbed," and to once more have his welcome contribution to our columns. Eds.]

www.ingramcontent.com/pod-product-compliance
Lightning Source LLC
LaVergne TN
LVHW081355060426
835510LV00013B/1840